SCIENCE EXPLORER

JUNIOR

JUNIOR SCIENTISTS

Experiment with Solar Energy

by Christine Taylor-Butler

CHERRY LAKE PUBLISHING · ANN ARBOR, MICHIGAN

Published in the United States of America by Cherry Lake Publishing
Ann Arbor, Michigan
www.cherrylakepublishing.com

Content Editor: Robert Wolffe, EdD, Professor of Teacher Education, Bradley University, Peoria, Illinois
Reading Adviser: Cecilia Minden-Cupp, PhD, Literacy Consultant

Design and Illustration: The Design Lab

Photo Credits: Page 10, ©iStockphoto.com/Mlenny; page 15, ©iStockphoto.com/attator; page 16, ©AdamEdwards/Shutterstock, Inc.; page 22, ©Julia Pivovarova/Shutterstock, Inc.; page 23, ©matka_Wariatka/Shutterstock, Inc.; page 27, ©evan66/Shutterstock, Inc.

Library of Congress Cataloging-in-Publication Data
Taylor-Butler, Christine.
  Junior scientists. Experiment with solar energy / by Christine Taylor-Butler.
    p. cm.—(Science explorer junior)
  Includes bibliographical references and index.
  ISBN-13: 978-1-60279-840-3 (lib. bdg.)
  ISBN-10: 1-60279-840-0 (lib. bdg.)
  1. Solar energy—Experiments—Juvenile literature. 2. Science projects—Juvenile literature. I. Title. II. Title: Experiment with solar energy. III. Series.
  TJ810.3.T389 2010
  621.47078—dc22   2009048823

Portions of the text have previously appeared in *Super Cool Science Experiments: Solar Energy* published by Cherry Lake Publishing.

Cherry Lake Publishing would like to acknowledge the work of The Partnership for 21st Century Skills. Please visit *www.21stcenturyskills.org* for more information.

Printed in the United States of America
Corporate Graphics Inc.
July 2010
CLFA07

TABLE OF CONTENTS

Let's Experiment!

Science is fun!

Have you ever done a science **experiment**? They can be a lot of fun! You can use experiments to learn about almost anything.

Scientists like to observe the world around them.

This book will help you learn how to think like a scientist. Scientists have a special way of learning new things. Some people call it the Scientific Method. This is how it often works:

- Scientists notice things. They **observe** the world around them. They ask questions about things they see, hear, taste, touch, or smell. They come up with problems they would like to solve.

A scientist guesses what the answer to his question might be.

- They gather information. They use what they already know to guess the answers to their questions. This kind of guess is called a **hypothesis**.

- Then they test their ideas. They perform experiments or build models. They watch and write down what happens. They learn from each new test.

Scientists perform experiments to answer their questions.

- They think about what they learned and reach a **conclusion**. This means they come up with an answer to their question. Sometimes they **conclude** that they need to do more experiments!

When a scientist figures out the answer to his question, he has reached a conclusion.

Let's think like scientists to find out if plants use sunlight.

We will think like scientists to learn more about **solar** energy. The sun gives energy to Earth. It gives us heat. It also lets us see what is around us. Have you ever wondered why we are warmer when we wear certain colors? How do plants use sunlight? How does solar energy affect water? We can do experiments to answer these questions and more. Each experiment will teach us something new. Are you ready to be a scientist?

Up, Up, and Away!

How does sunlight keep us warm?

What do we already know about solar energy? You know that the sun gives us light. It also gives us heat. Energy from the sun keeps Earth warm. Scientists know that different colors **absorb** different amounts of energy.

Which colors absorb the most solar energy? An experiment can help us find out. First, we need to choose a hypothesis:

1. Dark colors absorb more solar energy.
2. Light colors absorb more solar energy.

Let's get started!

Write down your hypothesis.

My hypothesis: Dark colors absorb more solar energy.

Here's what you'll need:

- 2 paintbrushes
- 2 clear plastic bottles
- 1 jar of black paint
- 1 jar of white paint
- 1 black balloon
- 1 white balloon

Collect your supplies.

Instructions:

1. Use one brush to paint one bottle black.
2. Use the other brush to paint the other bottle white.
3. Set the bottles aside until the paint dries.

Be careful! You don't want to get paint on your clothes.

Record what you see after 10 minutes.

4. Put the opening of the black balloon on the neck of the black bottle.

5. Put the white balloon on the neck of the white bottle.

6. Set the bottles on a sunny windowsill. Wait 10 minutes. What happens to the balloons?

Conclusion:

What happened to the balloons? Did both fill with air? Which balloon started to fill up first?

The darker bottle absorbed more solar energy. That energy heated the air inside the bottle. As the air got warmer, it was able to spread out more. As it spread out, it blew up the balloon. Does this explain your results? Was your hypothesis correct?

It's a good idea to wear light colors on hot, sunny days.

Clean Water from Solar Power

Can you see the steam rising from these pots?

Have you ever seen steam rising from a pot of very hot water? Water turns into a gas when it gets hot. This is called **evaporation**. Most evaporation happens because of heat from solar energy.

Raindrops start out as water on Earth. Water evaporates into the sky. Then it turns into rain. Raindrops are made of water that is mostly clean. But a lot of water on Earth is dirty. How does the water get clean? Do solar energy and evaporation have anything to do with it? Let's find out by doing an experiment. Here are some possible hypotheses:

1. Solar energy can make dirty water clean.

2. Solar energy cannot make dirty water clean.

Let's get started!

Solar energy cannot make dirty water clean.

What do you think will happen? Write it down.

Here's what you'll need:

- Coarse black pepper and other spices
- 1 tablespoon of soil
- 1 spoon
- 1 large glass of water
- 1 coffee cup
- 1 clear mixing bowl
- Plastic food wrap
- Rubber bands
- 1 small rock

Find all of your supplies.

Instructions:

1. Mix the pepper, spices, and soil into the glass of water. Stir until it is no longer clear.

2. Place the coffee cup in the center of the mixing bowl.

3. Pour the dirty water into the bowl. The water should reach just below the edge of the cup. Do not get water inside the cup.

Fill the bowl with the dirty water, making sure it doesn't go into the coffee cup.

Record what happens in 24 hours.

4. Cover the bowl with plastic wrap. Do not stretch it tight. It should give a little. Poke the plastic wrap with your finger in the area above the empty cup to make a dip. Do not make a hole. Use rubber bands to hold the plastic wrap on the bowl.

5. Place the rock in the dip of the plastic wrap. This will be a weight. The plastic wrap should dip down toward the cup without touching it.
6. Set the bowl next to a sunny window. Check it in 24 hours. Has anything changed? Record your observations.

Conclusion:

You should see water drops on the bottom of the plastic wrap. You should also see water in the coffee cup. Solar energy heated the water. Some of the water evaporated. The evaporated water cooled and turned back to liquid when it touched the plastic. The spices and soil did not evaporate. They stayed in the bowl. The water that dripped into the cup was clean. Solar energy helped clean the water! Was your hypothesis correct?

How Does Your Garden Grow?

Do plants need sunlight?

Solar energy is very important to farmers. They grow plants in places with sunlight. Why do you think they do this? Do you think plants need sunlight to grow? What happens if plants do not get any sunlight? These questions can be answered with a simple experiment. Start by picking a hypothesis:

1. Green plants need sunlight to stay healthy.
2. Green plants do not need sunlight to stay healthy.

Let's get started!

Plants need water.

Here's what you'll need:

- 2 small, green plants of the same kind and size. Bean plants work well.
- 2 glass jars of the same size
- Small pebbles
- Potting soil
- Water

Make sure your plants look green and healthy before you begin.

POTTING SOIL

Fill the bottom of each jar with pebbles and then add the soil.

Instructions:

1. Fill each jar with a 1-inch (2.5 centimeters) layer of pebbles.
2. Pour 2 inches (5.0 cm) of soil on top of the pebbles in each jar.
3. Make small holes in the soil. Then place one plant in each jar.

Record what you see every day for 10 days.

4. Add just enough water to each jar to make the soil moist. Make sure the soil stays moist, but not soggy, during the experiment.
5. Place one jar near a sunny window.
6. Place the other jar in a warm, dark closet.
7. Look at the jars every day for 10 days. Observe the plants. How do they look?

Conclusion:

How have the plants changed? Does the plant in the dark look different from the one in the light? Does it seem healthy? You can tell by the color of its leaves. Healthy plants have green leaves. Unhealthy ones have yellow or brown leaves. Green plants cannot live or grow for very long without sunlight. They need it to make their food. Was your hypothesis correct?

It is easy to spot an unhealthy plant.

Do It Yourself!

Can you think of other experiments you can do?

Okay, scientists! Now you know some things about solar energy. You learned that dark colors absorb more solar energy than light ones. You also learned that solar energy can be used to clean water. Finally, you learned that green plants need solar energy to live. You learned these things through your observations and experiments.

Do you have more questions about solar energy? Maybe you want to know if you can use solar energy to cook food. You might want to know if the color red absorbs more heat from the sun than the color blue. Try using the scientific method to answer your questions about solar energy!

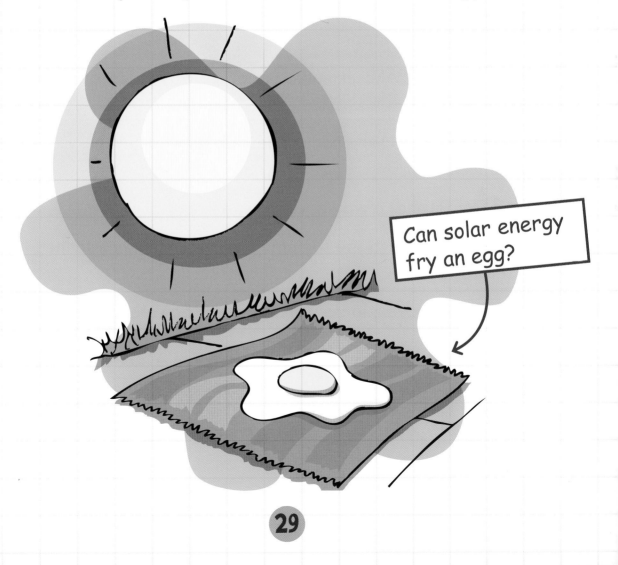

Can solar energy fry an egg?

GLOSSARY

absorb (ab-ZORB) to soak up

conclude (kuhn-KLOOD) to make a final decision based on what you know

conclusion (kuhn-KLOO-zhuhn) a final decision, thought, or opinion

evaporation (i-vap-uh-RAY-shuhn) the process in which a liquid changes to a gas or vapor

experiment (ecks-PARE-uh-ment) a scientific way to test a guess about something

hypothesis (hy-POTH-uh-sihss) a guess about what will happen in an experiment

method (METH-uhd) a way of doing something

observe (uhb-ZURV) to see something or notice things with the other senses

solar (SOH-lur) having to do with the sun or powered by the sun's energy

FOR MORE INFORMATION

BOOKS

Landau, Elaine. *The Sun*. New York: Children's Press, 2008.

Walker, Niki. *Harnessing Power from the Sun*. New York: Crabtree Publishing Company, 2007.

WEB SITES

**Energy Information Administration—
Energy Kid's Page: Solar Energy**
*www.eia.doe.gov/kids/energyfacts/sources/renewable/
solar.html#fromthesun*
Find more information about solar energy and its uses.

U.S. Department of Energy—Roofus' Solar & Efficient Home
www1.eere.energy.gov/kids/roofus/
Click on parts of a virtual home to find out how it uses solar energy.

INDEX

ABOUT THE AUTHOR

Christine Taylor-Butler is a freelance author with degrees in both civil engineering and art and design from MIT. When Christine is not writing, she is reading, drawing, or looking for unusual new science ideas to try. She is the author of more than 40 fiction and nonfiction books for children.